There Was An Old Fellow From Skye

Antony Wootten

Eskdale Publishing
England

www.antonywootten.co.uk

There Was An Old Fellow From Skye

Ode to Limericks

The task of a limerick poet,
Is tough, though we try not to show it.
The rhyme's the priority,
And then there is jollity,
With rhythm a short way below it.

When trying to tell you a story,
That's funny, romantic or gory,
Attempts to abridge it,
Will cause us to fidget,
Betraying frustration and fury.

A limerick tells of a scene,
Which often is crude or obscene.
But if smut's what you're after,
To bring about laughter,
Then tough, because these are all clean.

I've cobbled together these pages,
In order to add to my wages.
They're modest in size,
They'll win me no prize,
But smile, 'cause they've taken me ages.

There was an old fellow from Skye
Who told me that he was a spy,
Which wasn't the case;
You could tell by his face,
And his not inconspicuous tie.

There was an old fellow called Noakes
Who told the most terrible jokes.
Some were so awful
I doubt they were lawful;
They traumatised fully grown blokes.

A wigmaker known as Carruthers
Was terribly thoughtful to others.
He'd use his own hairs
When creating his wares
And then offer them free to young mothers.

An army-musician named Carp
Invented a deadly new harp.
He took it to war
And fought Zulu and Boer,
By playing them songs in F sharp.

I'm not sure this story is true:
It's said that a woman named Sue
Had ears like a rabbit's
And legs like a crab, it's
The source of a legend or two.

There once was a fellow named Hicks
Who trained his pet dog to do tricks.
Not the usual kind;
Jedi ones, of the mind.
Now Hicks is the one fetching sticks.

There once was a fellow from Beverley
Who swung from the ceiling, quite cleverly,
Whilst juggling sabres,
Astounding the neighbours.
"And now it's your turn," he said, levelly.

There once was a fellow named Platt-
Orange-Cake-Wildebeest-Hat-
Bottomly-Mop-
Tangleweed-Plop.
At least, it was something like that.

They say there's a farmer from Surrey
Who gets all the bits for his curry
From underneath slabs,
Or from bottles in labs,
Which is why he produces great slurry.

There once was a fellow from Yately
Who everyone thought of as stately.
But some of his habits
Were horrid for rabbits,
And changed my opinion greatly.

A gifted orator from Sicily
Was impaired by his voice which was whistly.
A word with an 'S'
Caused his audience stress
As their bodily hairs became bristly.

A vain little fellow named Miles
Developed a range of cute smiles.
But the effort it took
To create such a look
Was the cause of his terrible piles.

A clumsy young builder named Britt
Constructed some flats from a kit,
But lost the instructions,
And so his construction
Goes down and not up, like a pit.

There once was a woman named Pru
Who took her young son to the zoo.
A sign gently pleaded,
"Donations are needed."
She said, "Here's my son. Will that do?"

A fellow who came from Seahouses
Invented self-fastening blouses.
But often they'd tighten
So much you would whiten.
Thank goodness he didn't make trousers.

A boomerang maker named Wayne
Mistakenly took the wrong train.
At the very next station,
Just like his creation,
He turned and came homeward again.

A poet, the great Rimmer-Hicks,
Would oft' find himself in a fix.
He would jump up and down,
Sometimes run through the town,
Seeking endings for his… rhyming poems.

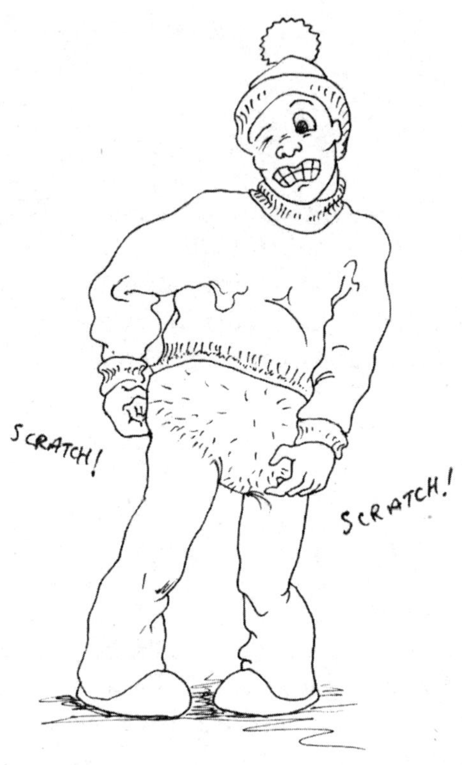

A loft insulator from Hants
Had quite a peculiar stance.
The reason, I'm told,
Is that when it grew cold
He had loft insulated his pants.

A beachcombing fellow named Bing
Found an incredible thing.
Its worth you could measure
By gauging the pleasure
It gave when it started to sing.

A demon who came from below
Went for skiing and fun to Oslo.
But the fires of Hades
Repelled all the ladies,
And instantly melted the snow.

A gardening expert named Royal
Grew a grotesque looking boil.
It was not on his face,
But a more private place:
His greenhouse, in well watered soil.

A ghost by the name of McGraw
Longs to haunt room a hundred and four.
But whenever he dares
To ascend flights of stairs,
He slips, with a sigh, through the floor.

There lived far away in the East
An ugly, though courteous beast,
Who moaned, with a roar,
"Would the girls like me more
If my trousers weren't terribly creased?"

A vampire, hunting alone,
Gave a blood-curdling moan,
But got quite annoyed
When the scene was destroyed
By the sound of his cellular phone.

A monster who longed to be scary
And terrify people called Mary,
Ran out of the house
At the sight of a mouse,
Shouting, "Help me! It's little and hairy!"

There once was a fellow from Gwent
Who wrote a short verse, and it went:
"A fellow named Clyde
Lived his life and then died."
But nobody knew what it meant.

A blacksmith whose surname is Marx
Competes in short races round parks.
But his shoes, which aren't leather,
Corrode in damp weather
And generate showers of sparks.

There once was a man from West-Widgeon
Who reared a talkative pigeon.
He offered it bread
And it cooed, and it said,
"Oh go on then, give us a smidgen."

There once was a fellow from Ayr
Who used to keep things in his hair
Like apples for lunch,
A glass of fruit punch
And in case he got weary, a chair.

A green, bug-eyed monster from space
Tripped and fell flat on his face.
Although he was here
To generate fear,
He had to go home in disgrace.

An aeroplane pilot called Lee
Always flew with a goat on his knee.
On a flight down to Spain
The goat flew the plane,
And still produced milk for their tea!

Some mice in a lab in Kirkain
Were put through great torment and pain.
But the drugs in their feed
Meant they learned how to read
And escaped by constructing a plane.

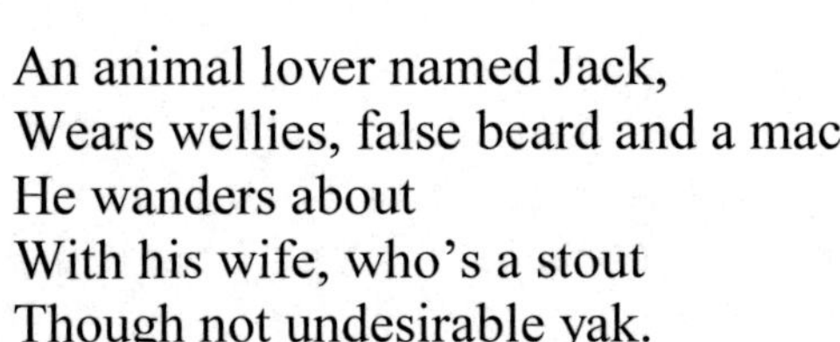

An animal lover named Jack,
Wears wellies, false beard and a mac.
He wanders about
With his wife, who's a stout
Though not undesirable yak.

There was an old fellow from Tring
Whose trousers were held up with string,
Which happened to break
When he stood up to make
A speech to the queen and the king.

There once was a fellow name Morse
Who swallowed a whopping great horse.
He then ate the rider
And, now slightly wider,
Was ready to start the main course.

There once was a fellow named Moon
Who ate living snakes in late June.
He said with a smile,
"Since they writhe all the while
They're tricky to get on the spoon."

Julie, a friend of a friend,
Cleaned lavatories at the weekend.
Whenever she rushed
She'd get awfully flushed,
And was thought to be clean round the bend.

Clumsy Sir Tristan, from France,
Invited his love to a dance.
In a bid to impress
The delightful princess,
He ran himself through with a lance.

A very strange surgeon named Wheeze
Removed patients' legs at the knees.
He said, "There's no doubt,
I have cured them of gout!"
Lord knows how he handled a sneeze.

A jockey I knew of named Bowes
Rode mammoths he found and de-froze.
It startled the horses
At various courses
And usually won by a nose.

I know of a fellow named Bill
Who makes body noises at will.
At parties with friends,
He quite often offends
With a sound that can make people ill.

There is a young fellow named Grant
Who says, "Yes there are," when there aren't.
It's really frustrating
To hang around waiting
For one who says, "Shall," meaning, "Shan't."

A clever inventor called Max
Makes cars that can run on earwax.
You don't need to mine it,
Or oil-refine it,
And he can provide it in sacks.

Arthur and all of his knights
Frequently got into fights,
'Til they started to learn
They must all take their turn
To wear Lady Guinevere's tights.

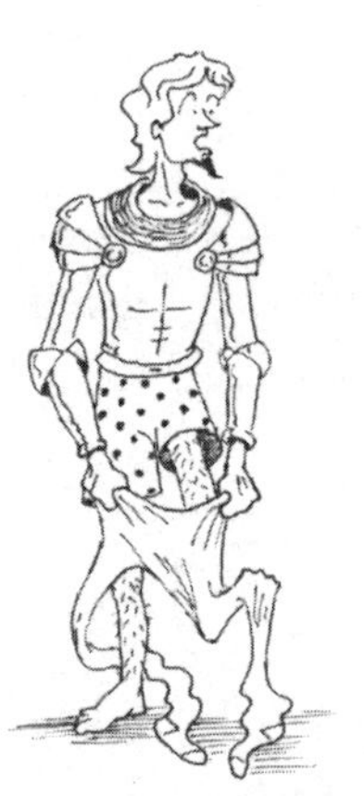

There once was a fellow named Reece
Who used to throw things at the geese.
One day, just for fun,
He threw cakes and a bun,
Four erasers, a dog and his niece.

Of crocodiles, Joe had a farmful.
He told me, "They're really not harmful."
Which seemed true at first,
But they harboured a thirst
For his blood, and one day took an armful.

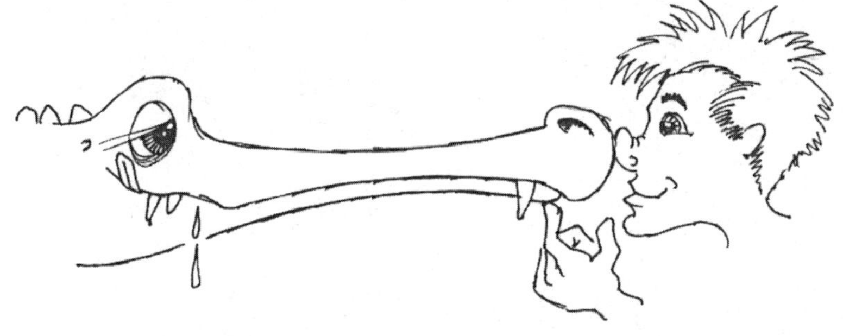

Jack, who had no airs or graces,
Would jump on young girls from high places.
But his end came about
When he jumped with a shout
And was caught on a branch by his braces.

A daring young climber from Kent
Would get funny looks when he went
To the neighbourhood store,
As he crawled on the floor
With his crampons, some rope and a tent.

There once was a dastardly fellow
Who came across all shy and mellow,
But really was barmy:
He had his own army
And planned to paint everything yellow.

When Zondor, a little green man,
Visited Earth with a plan
To form an alliance,
And help us with science,
They took him away in a van.

There once was a fellow from Harting
Who said to me one day, "I'm starting
A diet of beans
And of all kinds of greens!
The trouble is I keep… running out of recipe
ideas."

A fellow named Vincent Van Gogh
Had one of his ears cut off,
Though the barber, Pierre,
Had said, "Vincent, beware,
It's important you try not to cough."

There once was a guy from the States
Who couldn't stop hurdling gates.
He'd other odd trends
Which offended his friends
And ruined a lot of his dates.

There once was a magical bloke
Who could get rid of unwanted folk.
A neighbour named Mark,
Was last seen in the park,
And his wife, they say, went up in smoke.

There once was a fellow named Bright
Who sang like a banshee at night
From the roof of his flat,
'Til he tripped on the cat,
Who quietly purred, "Serves 'im right."

A fisherman fellow named Brett
Finds very odd things in his net:
A boot from a thug
And a powerful tug,
But he hasn't found any fish yet.

Sight Seeing Tours, Planet 3,
Plenty to do, modest fee.
Must hurry, book fast,
Ecosystem won't last,
Pollution destroying the sea.

There once was a fellow named Bysshe
Who served up a meal of fish.
It was utterly raw
As his visitors saw
When the starter swam twice round the dish.

There once was a boy called Aladdin
Who'd frequently walk about clad in
His shirt, brightly dyed,
And his trousers so wide
They could fit both his mum and his dad in.

Rapunzel, (whose hair was a dreadlock),
Persuaded the prince into wedlock.
'Twas not her cute grin
Which had suckered him in,
But the fact she had him in a headlock.

Delightfully innocent Jude
Ran happily round in the nude,
'Til a voice filled with rage
Bellowed, "Not at your age
Mother! Come in and finish your food."

I know of a farmer named Ken
Who married his favourite hen.
The locals declare,
When discussing the pair,
She has terribly bad taste in men.

There once was a fellow named Richie
Who spent a whole day feeling itchy.
Alas, when he found
The flee hopping around
It was most disappointingly titchy.

A very large sailor named Planket
Purchased a speedboat, and sank it.
It's clear that he oughta
Have drowned in the water,
But no. He just lay there and drank it.

St George spent the bulk of his life
Fighting dragons with dagger and knife.
Though known as a mighty
And powerful knight, he
Was terribly scared of his wife.

A couple of fellows named Wright
Would stay in the shed day and night.
The hammering sound
Made rumours abound,
'Til at last they emerged and took flight.

That infamous king, Henry Tudor,
Met Anne Boleyn, and he wooed her,
Then chopped off her head.
"More efficient," he said,
"Than if I had merely sued her."

A porcelain dealer named Banks
Paid the old man and said, "Thanks."
With a critical eye
He admired his buy:
A rare piece by Armitage Shanks.

There once was a man with a goat,
Two rabbits, four hens and a stoat,
Which he'd loved all his life
But it niggled his wife,
So he set her adrift in a boat.

There was an old lady called Myrtle
Whose favourite thing was to hurtle
Down mountains, off piste,
(Or a staircase at least)
Riding an overturned turtle.

A very large lady from Dorset
Has built a mechanical corset,
Complete with a pulley
To tighten it fully,
And brackets to help reinforce it.

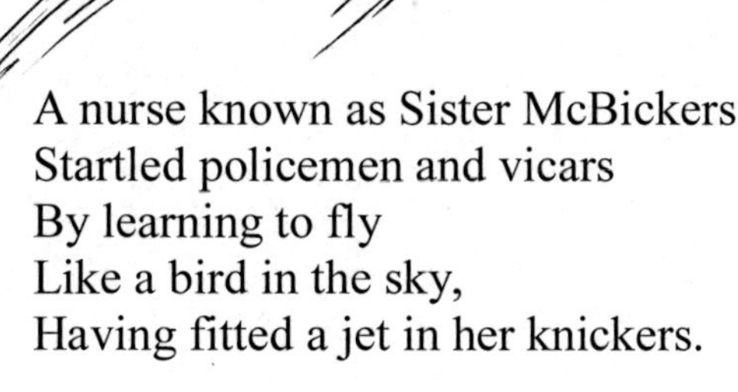

A nurse known as Sister McBickers
Startled policemen and vicars
By learning to fly
Like a bird in the sky,
Having fitted a jet in her knickers.

A feisty young fellow named Bertie
Told jokes in the pub that were dirty.
But whenever his friend did
He'd act all offended,
And go home and sulk at eight-thirty.

There once was a teacher from Goring
Whose lessons were terribly boring.
But nobody knew
Of the mad things he'd do
While his pupils were quietly snoring.

A spaceman's apprentice named Shaft
Was practising in his spacecraft.
Despite engines roaring
It stayed in its mooring:
He'd forgotten the handbrake. How daft.

There once was a fellow called Frank
Who fell in a river and sank.
Then came a pause
And a little applause
From the crowd which had formed on the bank.

There once was a fellow named Fox
Who packed himself into a box,
And positioned himself
In a shop on a shelf,
But was found by the smell of his socks.

Robin Hood said to Maid Marion,
"This is the hill we shall marry on."
But on their big day
They could not find the way.
What a mess, what a farce, what a carry-on.

A daft, one-eyed sous chef named Guy
Once tripped and fell into a pie.
A day or two later,
A diner said, "Waiter,
I think I've just found a glass eye."

There was an old fellow from Hayes
Who could burp in two quite different ways.
One way was smelly,
But got him on telly;
The other one started a craze.

An odd little fellow named Sam
Developed a thing about ham.
He'd purchase a shoulder
The size of a boulder
And push it around in a pram.

A sea-faring groom and his bride
Were to marry upon a high tide.
Though consumed by a whale
They cried, "Love must prevail!"
And the wedding continued, inside.

An old lighthouse keeper, named Drew
Had only one pet: a gnu.
They had good times aplenty,
As many as twenty!
And frequently shared a fondue.

A fishmonger's girlfriend named Grace
Had quite an incredible face.
She'd whiskers, like dog-fish,
And lumps, like a hog-fish,
And eyes on one side, like a plaice.

There was a mechanic called Bruce
Who made his car run on fruit juice.
It cured many ills,
Such as rust in the sills,
But its valves became terribly loose.

There once was a woman named Hughes
Who liked to go out buying shoes.
'Twas the source of some mirth
That a problem since birth
Meant she bought them in threes and not twos.

A fellow from Surrey named Vaughan
Emitted one heck of a yawn:
The rushing of air
Stripped his grandmother bare,
And propelled her the length of the lawn.

For two years, a chap called Jerome
Was lost in a car park in Frome.
Forgotten, outcast,
He survived, 'til at last
He located his car and drove home.

There once was a fellow named West
Who grew a third arm from his chest.
It made him a star,
People came from afar
Just to laugh at his ill-fitting vest.

A pretty inventor named Brenda
Could not find a man to befriend her,
So built one from pencils
And kitchen utensils,
But sadly it fancied the blender.

There once was a fellow named Brown
Who had to avoid bending down,
Because of the noise
That would scare little boys,
And anger the folk of the town.

The people of Alpha-Centauri
Are prone to surprise bouts of fury.
They've other odd trends
Such as kicking their friends,
And some of them even vote Tory.

William Shakespeare, playwright,
Said to his agent, "I may write
Some plays about kings
And some sonnets and things,
Using phrases that no-one can say right."

There once was a man from Argyll
Who dressed in his own unique style.
If he wore clothes at all,
They were always too small,
But mainly he just wore his smile.

A pilot who came from Dubai
Discovered a new way to fly.
A nail in his chair
Helped him take to the air,
Emitting a terrible cry.

A government agent called Brian
Barely could put his own tie on.
Cuff-links confused him
And braces bemused him,
Which made him quite funny to spy on.

There once was a fellow named Price
Who was terribly fond of his mice
Which he kept in a cage
'Til their coming of age;
Then he fried them and ate them with rice.

A girl with one green and one red sock
Was tough as a layer of bedrock.
She once caught a bear
Who'd escaped from the fair
And wrestled it into a headlock.

A nervous young singer called Nell,
Sang like the chime of a bell.
But she'd empty the hall,
If the venue was small,
By making a terrible smell.

A very large waiter from Norway
Got himself stuck in a doorway.
If it is your wish
To get hit with a fish
By the manager, that is a sure way.

Limerick writing devours
Seconds and minutes and hours.
I've been here for ages
Completing these pages;
I've not even watered my flowers.

My fingers are starting to ache,
It's difficult staying awake.
My friends think I'm dead
And I've not made my bed,
Now I'm off to the shops for some cake.

Novels by Antony Wootten

A Tiger Too Many

Jill is deeply fond of an elderly tiger in London Zoo. But when war breaks out, she makes a shocking discovery. For reasons she can barely begin to understand, the tiger, along with many other dangerous animals in the zoo, is about to be killed. She vows to prevent that from happening, but finds herself virtually powerless in an adults' world. That day, she begins a war of her own, a war to save a tiger.

"Real edge-of-the-seat-stuff." TheBookbag.co.uk

Grown-ups Can't Be Friends With Dragons

Brian is always in trouble at school, and his home life is far from peaceful. So he often runs away to the cave by the sea where he has happy memories. But there is something else in the cave: a creature, lonely and confused. Together they visit another world where they find wonderful friends, but also deadly enemies.

"You'll love Brian. Anyone who has struggled with childhood will recognise how he's feeling." TheBookbag.co.uk

"A fast-paced and ultimately heart-warming tale. A lovely read for fathers and sons to share." LoveReading4Kids.co.uk

The Grubby Feather Gang

It is 1915, and George's father refuses to go and fight in the trenches of World War One. He is branded a coward, and George does not know what to think.

Worse still, the school bully hangs George upside-down from the hayloft, and the next day, George gets the cane! So, with a bit of help from Emma, a curious newcomer to the village, he decides to take daring and drastic revenge on both the bully and his teacher. But he could never have predicted what happens next...

"If subsequent titles are as good as this, ACHUKA will be happy to help promote them."
Achuka.co.uk

Season of the Mammoth

Trouble is brewing in the tribe. The people are divided. Some want to go to war against the wanderers who travel to their valley every year to hunt mammoths, but others see that the wanderers are dying out and need help. Geb and Tannash, the son and daughter of the tribal leader, along with their strange friend, Scrim, are caught in the middle as the tribe splits apart and turns on itself. Can they —*should* they – help defend the wanderers?

You can find out more at **www.antonywootten.co.uk**

Novels by Antony's father, Paul Wootten:

The Yendak

Christer has shared most of his young life with his cousin Sophie. But when Sophie becomes desperately ill, his aunt hopes that the sound of Christer's voice might help to bring her round. He visits, as promised, and embarks on a quest for the mind of his cousin, lost somewhere in another dimension. Following clues in her diary he plunges into a strange world of oppressed people, ruled by the Yendak, a cruel and violent race. If they find him, he will never get back home.

Whispers on the Wasteland

Tim has spent the last few years of his life travelling from place to place, following his father's job. He rarely stays long enough to make any friends, and now he's come to Wattleford where a patch of wasteland is marked for development. A natural playground for the children, it has, over the centuries, sheltered humans and wildlife among its trees and shrubs. Tim finds himself strangely in tune with the peoples of the past, but the town council has plans to develop the wasteland. Modern machines bring destruction and change, and Tim and his father are all that stand in their way.

You can find out more at **www.beaufordhouse.co.uk**.